Heart Strings

Isabella Hannig

BookLeaf Publishing

India | USA | UK

Presentation by *BookLeaf Publishing*

Web: www.bookleafpub.com

E-mail: info@bookleafpub.com

ISBN: 9789363305120

First edition 2024

The Therapist

I told her to flee,
To pack up her bags and forever leave.
To take her child,
So they could finally grieve.
The life they had endured,
All because of he.

I told her it wasn't her fault,
but she never seemed to believe,
that she was blameless for his anger
and his deceit.

I've seen this a thousand times,
yet I never can conceive,
how one could treat their family
with such animosity.

Her Friend

It's hard to tell whose friend or foe.
But I know she never deserved to be treated so.
Though I may never truly know,
why he controls her soul,
I know she has longed for the freedom
 she lost forever ago.

I miss my friend, a once vibrant presence she
was.
But now darkness shrouds her being,
instead of love.

She's not a fool, I tell her so.
He's simply a trickster,
one that convinced her, that he would fix her.

She didn't need fixed,
Though I always knew.
She was perfect through, and through.

I wish she could be free,
Free from he, if only
 we could find her cages key.

A Lovely Little Drug

He was my infatuation,
The prefect form of an intoxication.
The Drug, the prescription
For my lonely-hearts addiction.

He was my perfect form of fiction,
A fantasy, that spoke to me
with flawless diction.

My lifeline with no jurisdiction,
For he tore down my walls
and left me, in the most
vulnerable position.

If You Ever Hated Me

If you loathe me,
then why do you clothe me
in the fabrics of your legacy.

If you despise me,
Then why do you cry for me,
when you'd rather I lay down and die.
The victim of an oh-so-perfect demise.

If you abhor me,
then why do you deplore me,
when you for sure, would
rather me endure the wrath
of this world forevermore.

Just A Child

Was it just a dream,
or did
I hear my daddy scream?
Scream mean words at my mommy,
meant to demean.

Did I imagine it
when he thrashed her,
and lashed her, and left her crying
alone on the floor.
Or was it normal that I was worried she
wouldn't
wake up anymore.

I wished I wasn't so afraid of this family war.
Perhaps daddy was a nice man,
once before.
I only wish
I could restore, the peace lost
in my heart, forevermore.
And be the child I was meant
to be afore.

The Survivor

Blood on the floor,
you called me a whore.
And laughed
at my miseries, therefore
I should wish I wasn't so poor.
To suffer your wrath forevermore.

I pleaded for your mercy,
but a mockery of me
you made.
Perhaps you always
wished to see my heart fade,
and my body degrade.

Had I known the suffering
I would face,
I never would have treated you
with such grace.

Should freedom I find,
a place of my own in this world,
would finally be divine.

Him

She hasn't bled enough for me
today, Though I merely
wish to play. To make a painting
in her DNA,
and to crack her bones
like a guitar
when she dares to disobey.

To foster her little cries
when she can't
handle my delightful surprise.
To make a mockery of her pleas
while she begged
for mercy on her bloodied knees.

She's a little toy, she best know.
A puppet with a perfect
face that I could
never forgo.
I'm merciful, she must see.
Though I'll never tire
of hearing her delightful pleas.

Owned

You made me into your perfect antique.
Displaying me as your tamed little freak.
You called me meek, and weak.
Promising that my life without you
would be quite bleak.

And yet I knew without you,
I could be something unique.
A powerful person that no one,
even you, would dare to critique.

I wish I could have seen
how you could only mistreat.
If only I could find my voice,
and finally have the bravery,
to speak.

Death of a Soul

An opaque monster of fear shrouds my
darkness here. From a colorless soul I plead,
to let my poor heart bleed.

To allow the light in my body to never
leave. Lord save me please.
For a lightless life I cannot lead. I'm at
the mercy of the heavens, you must see.

Save the boy inside me, I plead,
or let me lay in my grave,
forever a boy left to bleed.
I'm a broken boy, now you must see.

The Perfect Body: A fairytale

Don't you see the painting on my skin?
They cover me in vibrant shades of
black, and blues and greys.
My body's a canvas,
where the abuse is the display.

See how my body crackles, and creaks.
Letting out its own, personal little shrieks.
As if it's screams, will save me from
the worst possible extremes.

Do you see the way I slump and slim.
My body becoming ever so,
paper thin.

Or do you lack to see through my veil,
that my perfectly crafted body,
was little more than a fairytale.

Your Convenience

Don't placate me, for I will know
if you whisper sweet words of nothing,
just for show.

Don't lie to me, nor shed fake tears
as you cry for me.
For I know, those tears
are as worthless as they go.

I know you care for me not.
I'm just a clot,
for your heart seems to bleed
black quite a lot.

And though I'm just a band-aid for your
self-inflicted wounds, I hate you
for once making me swoon.

My Treasure

You were my gold. Buried deep
within the treasures trove.
For I stole you to bring
to my hearts abode.
And bestowed upon you a love,
that shall never erode.

From heavens arms you came,
you turned my measly love for you,
into more than just a game.
You set me aflame.
And left me wishing to be tamed.

Like a moth drawn to a flame.
I was drawn to you since heaven came
and told me you were my love,
sent as a gift from destiny herself above.

Played the Fool

One upon a time,
I'd promised you'd be mine.
And bear a crown of gold,
that bore decades of fortunes untold.

I told you that you'd reign for years,
but only first if you could face your fears.
And be a woman that is forever revered,
by the peasants of the land, we cleared.

Little did I know, my love was never a desire,
you had. Even forever ago.
I was merely a tool, a fool!
So, you could be queen. And rule.

The Cruel King

My mask glistens gold.
A perfect picture to uphold.
Yet I never seem to fit the mold.
I was not one who could
be so easily controlled.

A creature unclaimed, untamed.
An animalistic desire for fame.
To uphold my birth-rights claim.
And be the name, in decades of stories,
all telling the same.

Telling of my wrath for the weak.
My lack of care for the meek.
And my wicked-ry reserved for only the most
unique.
The most unhinged of freaks.
Left to suffer something utterly,
perfectly, oblique.

Lost in Myself

I'm afraid of thread the monsters in my head,
for they unravel each and every thread.
Until I have nothing left to shed.
Do they truly wish to see me dead?
Or am I just feeling some sort of existential
dread.

Maybe it's all an illusion.
For my head can't seem
to overcome the pollution.
Maybe there simply isn't a solution.

Perhaps I'm just slowly
marching to my execution.
For my mind seems determined to kill,
if only I didn't forget to take my pills.

Burnt Out

Maybe I'm made of glass,
easily broken yet forged in fire.
Made to handle,
each and every one of your desires.

Maybe I was made to be shattered
and battered. Thrown aside,
like I never even mattered.

Perhaps it was my fault,
that you broke me.
And provoked me.

And left me picking up the,
pieces of myself on the floor.
Sometimes I wish I died long before.
Then I would have never suffered such
breaking pains afore.

Is My Rage Pretty to You

I'm not a pet.
What don't you get?
I won't slit, stay, or play.
I'm not some pretty little thing for
you to display.

Don't command me,
not demand me.
When you won't even make the simple effort
to understand me.

I won't be leashed.
So don't try to control me,
or uselessly console me.
When you rarely even mean the words that
roll off your forked tongue.

You call me the animal,
but a greater beast you are.
One who belongs in a cage,
maybe it will contain you,
like it once did my feminine rage.

Were you Ever Mine

Whisper lies to me one more time.
Let me delude myself into thinking your mine.
Give me a sign,
that your love was simply in decline.

Did I imagine it,
when you said you loved me,
and hugged me,
and promised me a lifetime with you.

Or were those sweet words no more
than a mirage.
A perfectly worded, woven collage.
So, you could execute your masterful barrage.
And wear my heart like a trophy,
one a perfectly made corsage.

Broken Ties

I'm your daughter not some swine.
Since when did you resign to
call me the wrench, witch, and the wicked bitch.
It's like you turned a switch.
Just to make me flinch and twitch.

Does it please you when I'm afraid,
my fear displayed.
For you to taunt and haunt.
Is my terror all you truly want?
Or is there something more
that you wish to flaunt?

Perhaps it pleased you to see me cower.
Made you feel some special sort of power.
Maybe you needed to see me break,
to heal, for your own sake.

Our Handmade Utopia

We built a dynasty,
a wondrous society,
on our shared anxiety.

We prayed our Kingdom would survive.
Designed it to forever thrive.
So long as we could remain alive,
and revive those before us who had once strived.

Strive to create a land of wonders.
A Home free of blunders.
A utopia made of a thousand, lovely miracles.

Star-Crossed

I missed you.
How I kissed you.
And reminisced with you.
Under the star-lite sky.

How I needed you,
for you completed me.
And treated me with such a
gentle kind of love.
As if you were my soulmate from above.
My slice of heaven, thereof.

I'll always cherish those nights
under the stars.
Where we shared our scars,
and fell forever in love.